# You Are My Sunshine

Adapted by Steve Metzger
Illustrated by Jill Dubin

SCHOLASTIC INC.  Cartwheel BOOKS®

New York  Toronto  London  Auckland  Sydney
Mexico City  New Delhi  Hong Kong  Buenos Aires

To Henry and Nina,
my rays of sunshine.
—J.D.

ISBN 0-439-26631-9

10                                                                                           03  04  05

Printed in the U.S.A.                                                           23
First printing, September 2001

You are my sunshine,
my only sunshine.

You make me happy,
when skies are gray.

You'll never know, dear,
how much I love you.

Please don't take
my sunshine away.

You are my starshine,
my only starshine.

I love you so much,
each night and day.

You'll never know, dear,
how much I love you.

Please don't take
my starshine away.

You are my loveshine,
my only loveshine.

I miss you so much,
when you're away.

You'll never know, dear,
how much I love you.

Please don't take
my loveshine away.

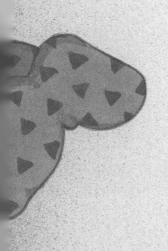

You are my sunshine,
my only sunshine.

You make me happy,
when skies are gray.

You'll never know, dear,
how much I love you.

Please don't take
my sunshine away.

# You Are My Sunshine

You are my sun - shine, _____ _____ my on - ly sun - shine. _____ _____ You make me hap - py, _____ _____ when skies are gray. _____ You'll nev - er know, dear, _____ _____ how much I love you. _____ Please don't take my sun - shine a - way. _____